W0377239

SO NUTZEN SIE DIESES THEMENHEFT

Die Stationen sind zum einen in die inhaltlichen Bereiche *Vorwissen, Immigration, Geography, Planning a Sightseeing Tour, A NYC Sightseeing Tour, Sports in NYC, Language Matters* und *Revision* untergliedert, zum anderen in die Bereiche *Vocabulary Exercises* und *Activities.* So ergibt sich folgende Übersicht:

Start and Finish		**Station A** Immigration	**Station B** Geography	**Station C** Planning a Sightseeing Tour	**Station D** A NYC Sightseeing Tour	**Station E** Sports in NYC	**Station F** Language Matters	**Station G** Revision
Part I								
Start/ Vorwissen: What I know about NYC (Mindmap)	Text	Text: Ellis Island – the Gateway to America	Text: New York – A City Full of Superlatives	Text: NYC Sightseeing Adverts	Listening: What the Guide tells You	Text: Baseball	Texts: A Short Message A Poem	
	Vocabulary Exercises	Completing a List: Nouns and Verbs	Finding Synonyms	Finding Adjectives	Completing a List: Nouns, Verbs, Adjectives	Idioms (Baseball Expressions)	Writing a Short Message and a Poem	
	Activities	Crossword Puzzle	Maze		Matching Sights and Descriptions	Matching Sentence Beginnings/ Questions and Endings/ Answers	Matching Word Triangles (American and British English)	Board Game: A Tour through NYC
Part II								
	Text	Listening: Emma's Registration Card	Texts (A/B): NYC and its Boroughs	Text: The Statue of Liberty		Text: The NYC Marathon		
	Activities	Filling in Registration Cards	Completing a Map	Game: Right and Wrong Statements	Game: Win with Adjectives	Marking the Marathon Route	Creating a NYC Acrostic	
Finish: What I know about NYC (Completing the Mindmap)			Completing a List/ Partner Interview	Practice: Translating Security Guidelines	Practice: Describing the Way	Answering Questions		Finish: What I know about NYC (Completing the Mindmap)
				Forming *if-clauses:* Planning a Tour				Feedback Filling in a Card: My Favourite Station

Ferner wurden die Stationen zur besseren Übersicht in Part I und II untergliedert. Die Arbeitsaufträge in *Part I* und *II* beziehen sich jeweils auf unterschiedliche Texte. Bei der Durchführung können jedoch die einzelnen Stationen unabhängig voneinander angeboten werden, wodurch es auch möglich ist, die Themengebiete auch in unterschiedlichem Umfang und mit unterschiedlichen Schwerpunkten zu behandeln.

Das Arbeitsblatt mit der Mindmap *What I know about New York City* (S. 5) bildet den Einstieg und den Abschluss des Stationenlernens über New York City. Die Schüler sollten die Mindmap vor Beginn ihrer Arbeit an den Stationen ausfüllen und nach Beendigung der letzten Station um ihr neu erworbenes Wissen ergänzen. Die Ergänzung am Ende sollte möglichst in einer anderen Farbe erfolgen, so dass der Wissenszuwachs für die Schüler auch visuell verdeutlich wird.

Die Schüler können die Sozialform (Einzel-, Partner- und Gruppenarbeit) im Allgemeinen frei wählen. Bei Stationen, die nur in Partnerarbeit durchgeführt werden können, enthält der Arbeitsauftrag entsprechende Hinweise.

Für die Durchführung des Stationenlernens empfiehlt es sich, dass die Schüler sich einen Schnellhefter mit linierten Blättern anlegen. Hier können sie die neuen Vokabeln eintragen und die ausgefüllten Arbeitsblätter sowie den Laufzettel abheften, so dass sie im Laufe des Stationenlernens eine eigene New-York-Mappe erstellen, die sie nach Belieben mit eigenen Materialien erweitern oder ergänzen können.

Es empfiehlt sich, die Arbeitsaufträge ein- oder zweifach zu kopieren, zu laminieren und an den Stationen bereitzustellen. Zur besseren Übersichtlichkeit für die Schüler sollten die Arbeitsaufträge aus einem Themenbereich je auf Bögen derselben Farbe kopiert werden, sofern man mit farbigem Papier arbeitet.

Die Lösungsblätter sollten getrennt von den Stationen, z. B. in einem Ordner, aufbewahrt werden.

Für die Stationen zum Bereich *Revision* empfiehlt es sich, ein Poster oder eine Übersicht im Klassenzimmer vorzubereiten, worauf die Schüler ihre Karten „My Favourite Station" und ihr „Acrostic" aus *Language Matters* anbringen oder direkt eintragen können. Auf diese Weise ergibt sich eine übersichtliche Grundlage für das gemeinsame Abschlussgespräch mit der Klasse.

Zur besseren Übersicht für die Lehrkraft über den Arbeitsverlauf der Schüler sollte (über den Laufzettel der Schüler hinaus) im Klassenraum ein großes Plakat mit den eingetragenen Stationennamen angebracht werden, auf dem die Schüler die bearbeiteten Stationen als erledigt markieren können. Gleichzeitig erleichtert diese Übersicht den Schülern die Partnersuche zur Bearbeitung der Aufgaben, die nur in Partnerarbeit gelöst werden können.

MATERIALIEN UND HINWEISE ZU DEN STATIONEN

(Wenn nicht anders angegeben, bitte je eine Kopie pro Schüler zur Verfügung stellen.)

LAUFZETTEL VON: ______________________________

Die folgenden Stationen habe ich schon geschafft:

WHAT I KNOW ABOUT NEW YORK CITY

New York City is full of famous sights we often see in movies or on television.

- **Before** you start working on the stations: Complete the mind map by writing down all the buildings, parks, museums, boroughs and interesting facts and figures that you already know.
- **After** you have finished all the stations: Have a look at your mind map once again. Use a different colour and add what you now know about New York City. Now compare: What was new for you?

Materials: mind map, two different writing colours

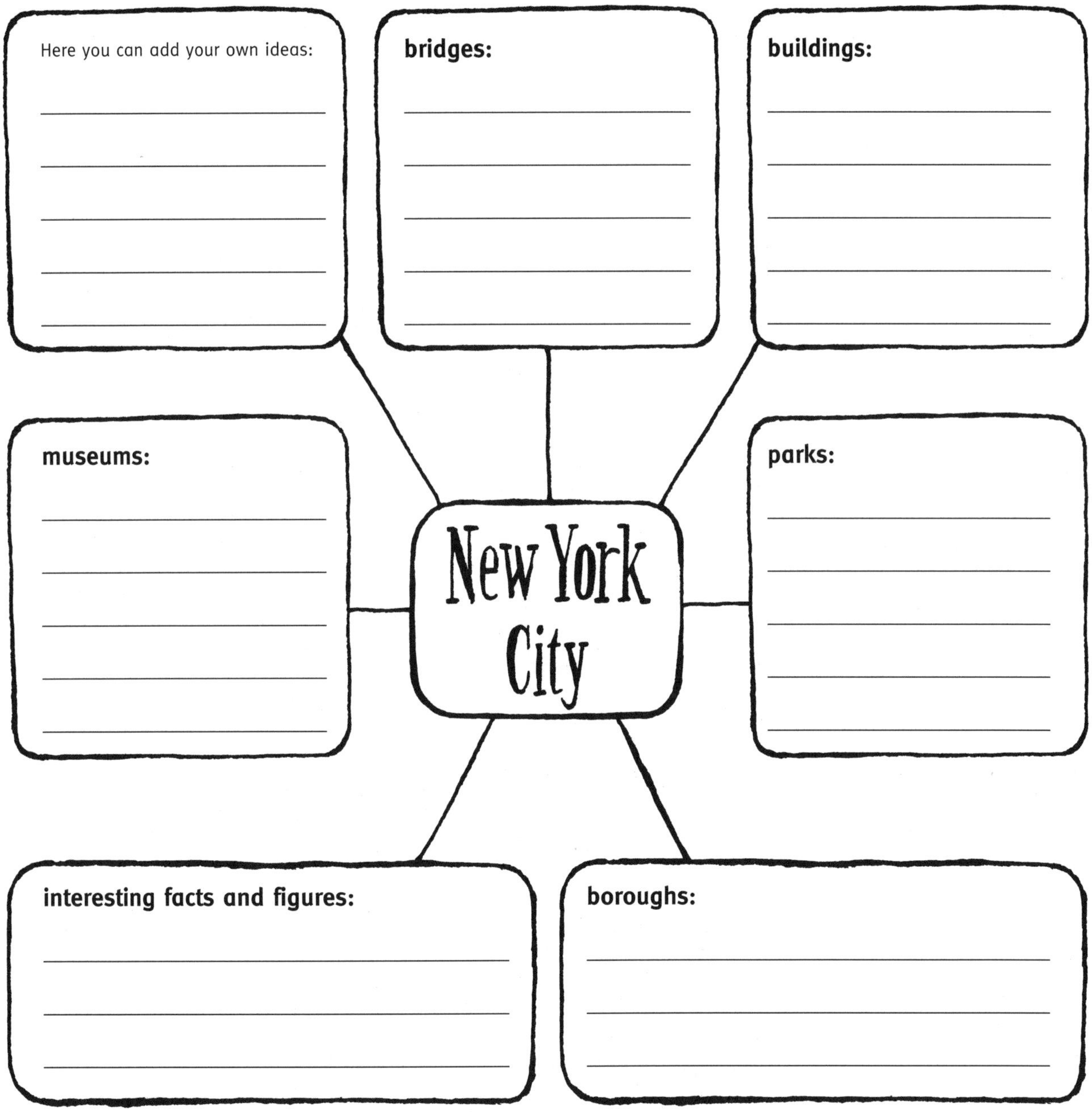

ELLIS ISLAND

Between 1892 and 1954 Ellis Island was the gateway to the USA for millions of immigrants who wanted to start a new life in the United States.

- Read the text about Ellis Island.
- Look up all the words you don't know in a dictionary and complete the vocabulary list (A2) by filling in the missing verbs and nouns. Compare your list with the answer key.
- Complete the crossword puzzle on your worksheet (A3) and compare your solution with the answer key.

Materials: text "Ellis Island ...", dictionary, worksheet A2 "vocabulary list" and answer key, worksheet A3 "Ellis Island crossword Puzzle" and answer key

Text: Ellis Island – the Gateway to America

For millions of immigrants New York Harbor was the gateway to the USA. When arriving on Ellis Island they were welcomed by the Statue of Liberty – a symbol of freedom and hope. Immigrants came to New York to escape from hunger or religious or political persecution in their home countries.

But after their arrival on Ellis Island they first had to go through the immigration process in the Registry Room, which opened on January 1, 1892. On its opening day 700 immigrants passed the registration process. The first was a 15-year-old girl from Ireland named Annie Moore. She came with her two brothers and wanted to follow her parents, who lived in Manhattan. Like all the other immigrants, Annie Moore had to go through a medical and mental check.

About two per cent of the immigrants who arrived here were sent back to their home country. One of the possible reasons why they had to return was a contagious disease* that could endanger public health, another was a criminal background. For those who were rejected Ellis Island became the "Island of Tears". But most immigrants were able to begin their new life in the state of hope only a few hours after their arrival. About twelve million people passed the immigration process in the Registry Room, which was closed on November 12, 1954. Today one of New York's most famous historical sights – the Ellis Island Immigration Museum – is housed in the same building that the immigrants once came through. Here you can see some of the immigrants' personal belongings** as for example suitcases, letters and registration cards.

**ansteckende Krankheit*

***persönliche Sachen*

WORKSHEET: VOCABULARY LIST

ENGLISH		GERMAN	
NOUN	VERB	NOUN	VERB
immigrant	*immigrate*	*Einwanderer*	*einwandern*
	arrive		ankommen
hope		Hoffnung	
	escape	Flucht	
persecution			verfolgen
	check		(über)prüfen
	return	Rückkehr	
	endanger	Gefahr	
	reject		ablehnen

ELLIS ISLAND CROSSWORD PUZZLE

1. ... came to America in search for a better life.
2. When the immigrants sailed to Ellis Island, they were welcomed by the ... ...
3. The first immigrant who arrived at Ellis Island came from ... .
4. Immigrants who had a contagious ... had to return to their home country.
5. Immigrants came to New York to escape from ... and religious or political persecution.
6. The Registry Room ... in 1892.
7. For millions of immigrants New York ... was the gateway to the USA.
8. The Statue of Liberty is a symbol of ... and hope.
9. Contagious diseases could endanger public ... .
10. Immigrants had to go through a medical and ... check.
11. The name of the first immigrant who arrived on Ellis Island: ... .
12. The immigration process started at this place.
13. One of New York's most famous historical sights is the Ellis Island Immigration ... .

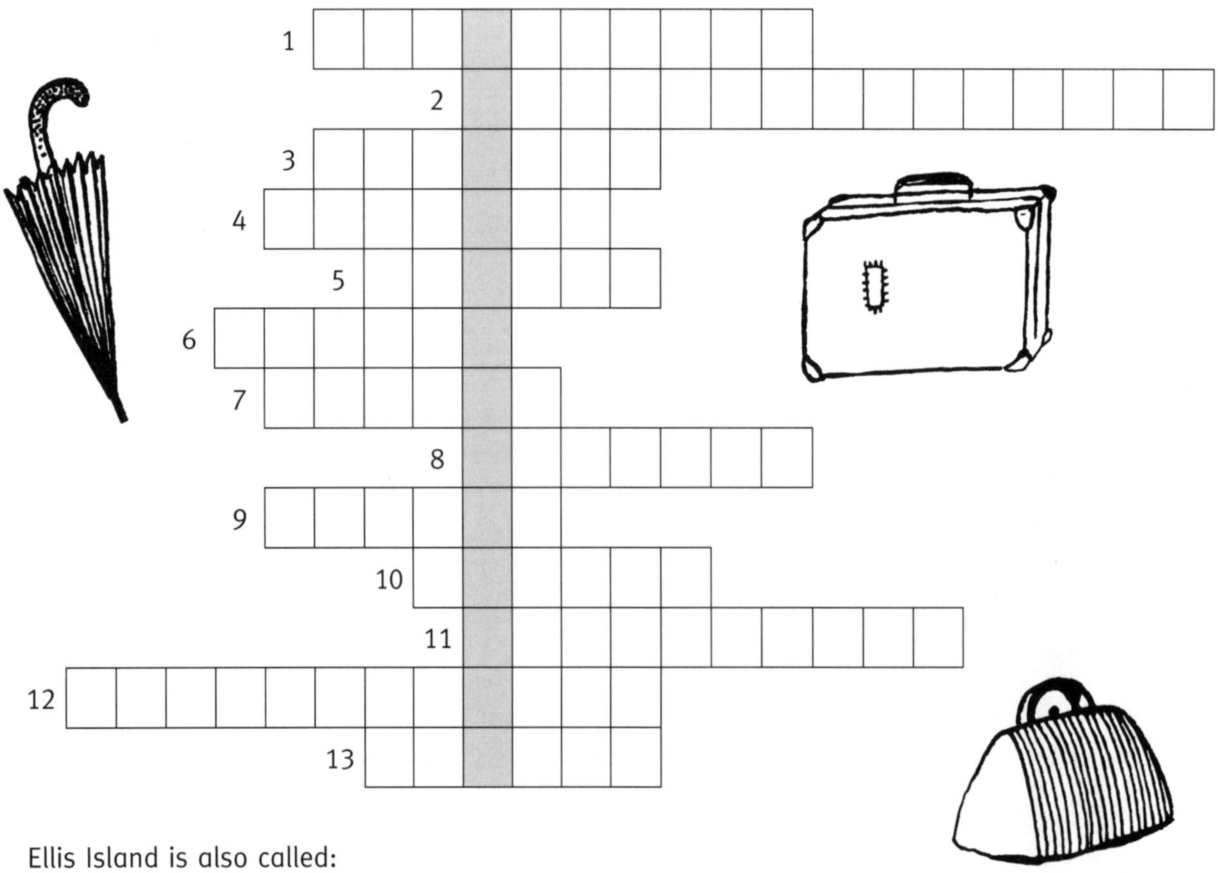

Ellis Island is also called:

___ ___ ___ ___ ___ ___ ___ ___ ___ ___ ___ ___ ___

1. 2. 3. 4. 5. 6. 7. 8. 9. 10. 11. 12. 13.

EMMA'S REGISTRATION CARD

Immigrants who came to Ellis Island had to go through an immigration process and were registered on registration cards.

- Listen to the story of Emma and look up any unknown words on the registration card.
- Listen to the story once again and fill in the registration card on your worksheet.
- Compare your solution with the answer key.
- Imagine you are an immigrant arriving on Ellis Island. Fill in your personal registration card on your worksheet.

Materials: cassette, cassette recorder, worksheet with two registration cards, answer key

My name is Emma Mac Gowan – Emma with double m and you spell Mac Gowan with a capital M, small a and c, then a capital G and small o-w-a-n. I was born on July 29, 1894 and I came to the USA from Connacht in Ireland. You spell Connacht with a capital C then o-double-n-c-h-t. In the country, where I grew up, a lot of people are poor. My grandmother still remembers the "Great Hunger". It was the time when almost a million Irish people died because they had nothing to eat. I love Ireland and I didn't want to leave my home country but we had no land and no work. Grandma had five brothers and two sisters. Both her sisters died. One of her brothers, Conor, came to America. He became a fireman in Manhattan. When I have settled, I am going to get a job in Manhattan too.

REGISTRATION CARD

Name: ______________________

First name: ______________________

Date of birth: ______________________

Last permanent residence:

Country: ______________________

Town: ______________________

Final destination: ______________________

Reason for leaving: ______________________

YOUR REGISTRATION CARD

Name: ______________________

First name: ______________________

Date of birth: ______________________

Last permanent residence:

Country: ______________________

Town: ______________________

Final destination: ______________________

Reason for leaving: ______________________

A CITY FULL OF SUPERLATIVES

- Read the text "A City Full of Superlatives".
- Look up the words you need in a dictionary.
- With the help of the text, find other expressions (= synonyms) for the underlined words on worksheet B2. Compare the words you have written down with the answer key.
- Answer the questions about the text and find the right words for the maze on worksheet B3. If you follow the words correctly, the letters in the grey squares will make up a popular dessert in America. You can go right →, left ← and down ↓.

Materials: text "New York City – a City Full of Superlatives", dictionary, worksheet B2 "Vocabulary: Synonyms" and answer key, worksheet B3 "A New York City Maze" and answer key

NEW YORK – A CITY FULL OF SUPERLATIVES

New York City is the largest city in the USA: over eight million people live in an area of 786 square kilometres which make up five boroughs. The most famous borough is Manhattan, often incorrectly used as a synonym for New York City because most of the tourist attractions can be found here. The inhabitants of the city area are called "New Yorkers".

New York City is one of the world's leading financial, business and cultural centers – it is full of superlatives: about 10,200 kilometres of streets and 1,300 kilometres of subway tracks lead the people through "the city that never sleeps". More than 500 galeries, 200 museums, 150 theatres and 18,000 restaurants attract tourists from all over the world. The cityscape of the "Big Apple" is dominated by skyscrapers and for forty years it has been the backdrop* to the world's tallest building, the Empire State Building.

The city has always been a main attraction for immigrants and is popular for its ethnic diversity: in 2007 nearly 170 languages were spoken in New York City and about 36 per cent of its population were born in a foreign country. Little Italy, Chinatown and Spanish Harlem are just a few examples of communities that represent the city's cultural diversity. In the 1980s New York City had a significant population growth caused by a new wave of immigration from Latin America, Asia, Jamaica, Haiti and Africa. Today most of New York's new immigrants still come from these countries.

*backdrop = *Hintergrund, Kulisse*

FINDING SYNONYMS

■ With the help of text B1, find other words (= synonyms) for the underlined words.

1. The most popular borough of New York City is Manhattan.

   most famous

2. Manhattan is often mistakenly used as another name for New York City.

3. About 1,300 kilometres of subway track guide the people through New York City.

4. The view of the city is dominated by tall buildings.

5. New York City is also famous for its ethnic variety.

6. About 36 per cent of New York's population were born in another country.

7. In the 1980s New York City had a population increase caused by a new wave of immigration.

A NEW YORK CITY MAZE

Facts about New York City:

1. Most of NYC's tourist attractions are located in this borough.
2. Manhattan is often used as a ______________ for NYC.
3. Its inhabitants are called ________________ .
4. Its nickname is ______________________________ .
5. Its cityscape is dominated by _____________________ .
6. In 2007 nearly ____________ languages were spoken in NYC and ... .
7. ... about 36 per cent of its population were born in a _______________ .
8. In the 1980s the city had a significant ____________________ .

Manhattan A	The Bronx L	antonym P	China Town D	immigrants S
synonym P	New Yorkers P	The Empire State Building G	180 A	subway F
ethnic diversity E	the Big Apple L	skyscrapers E	inhabitants N	museum S
Latin American I	150 H	170 P	foreign country I	population growth E
cityscape T	theatres M	community C	Little Italy T	boroughs H

A popular dessert in the USA: A ___ ___ ___ ___   ___ ___ ___

1. 2. 3. 4. 5.   6. 7. 8.

THE BOROUGHS OF NEW YORK CITY

- Work with a partner.
- Take the texts “New York City and its Boroughs”. One of you reads text A and the other one text B. Each text contains different information about the boroughs of New York City.
- Look up the words you do not know and write them down in your exercise book. (You and your partner may help each other.)
- Take worksheet B4. First, fill in the names of the boroughs. Compare your solution to the answer key.
- Second, fill in the table and use the facts given in your text.
- Ask your partner for the pieces of information missing in your text and complete your list. Compare your completed list with the answer key.

Materials: texts A and B “New York City and its Boroughs”, worksheet 3C “NYC and its Boroughs”, answer key

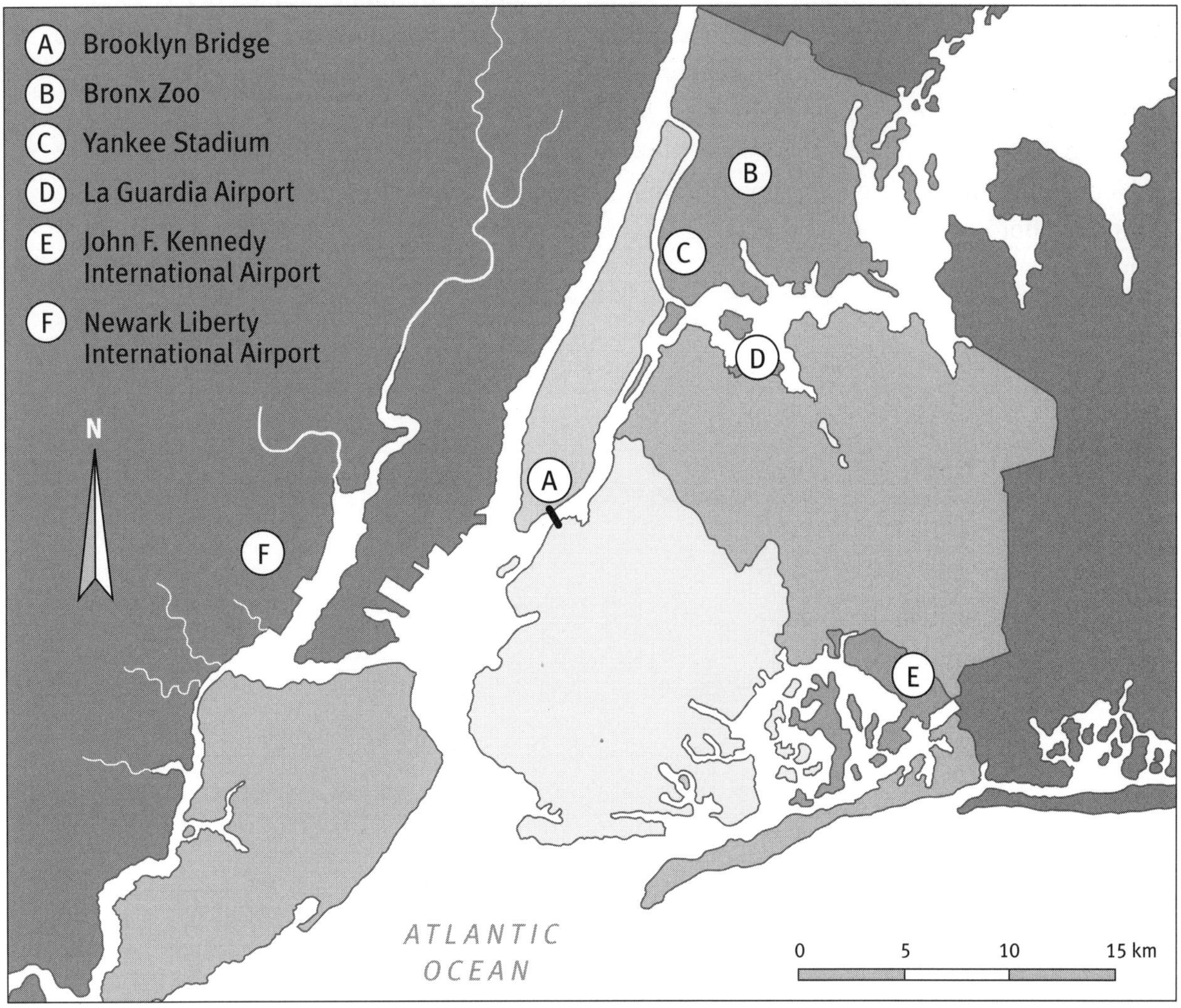

TEXT A

New York City and its Boroughs

New York City is made up of five boroughs: Brooklyn, Manhattan, Queens, Staten Island and The Bronx. **Brooklyn** is New York City's most populous borough although it is only the third largest in area. It covers about 251 square kilometres. Brooklyn is well-known for the Brooklyn Bridge. It connects Brooklyn to **Manhattan,** the most famous borough in New York City. Only 1.5 million people live in this borough, but as it is one of the smallest counties of the United States it is also one of the most densely populated. And this is not the only record – most of New York City's tourist attractions are located on this island, for example the Empire State Building. **Queens** is the largest borough in area: it covers about 462 square kilometres and is the second most populous of all five boroughs. Queens is home to John F. Kennedy Airport, the biggest international airport of the USA and Flushing Meadows Corona Park where the annual US Open tennis tournament takes place. **Staten Island** is by far the least populated borough: only 444 thousand people live there. The island is also called "the forgotten borough" because it is much less well known than the other four boroughs. The most famous attraction in this borough is the Staten Island Ferry that connects this island to lower Manhattan and goes past the Statue of Liberty. **The Bronx** covers an area of about 149 square kilometres and is the second biggest borough in area. The Bronx is also well known as the birthplace of rap and hip hop.

TEXT B

New York City and its Boroughs

New York City is made up of five boroughs: Brooklyn, Manhattan, Queens, Staten Island and The Bronx.
Brooklyn is New York City's most populous borough: nearly 2.5 million people live in the third largest borough in area. The most famous sight is the Brooklyn Bridge – it connects Brooklyn to **Manhattan,** the most famous county in New York City. Covering an area of only 88 square kilometres this borough is one of the smallest and most densely populated counties of the United States. But this is not the only record – most of New York City's tourist attractions are located on this island, for example The Empire State Building, The UN Building, Union Square and Central Park.
The largest borough in area is **Queens.** It has about 2.2 million inhabitants and is the second most populous of all five boroughs. **Staten Island** covers an area of about 266 square kilometres and is by far the least populated borough of New York City. This island is also called "the forgotten borough" because it is much less well known than the other four boroughs. About 1.4 million people live in the second smallest borough, **The Bronx.** Its attractions include the Yankee Stadium, home of the New York Yankees baseball club of the American League and the Bronx Zoo, the largest zoo in New York.

WORKSHEET: NEW YORK CITY AND ITS BOROUGHS

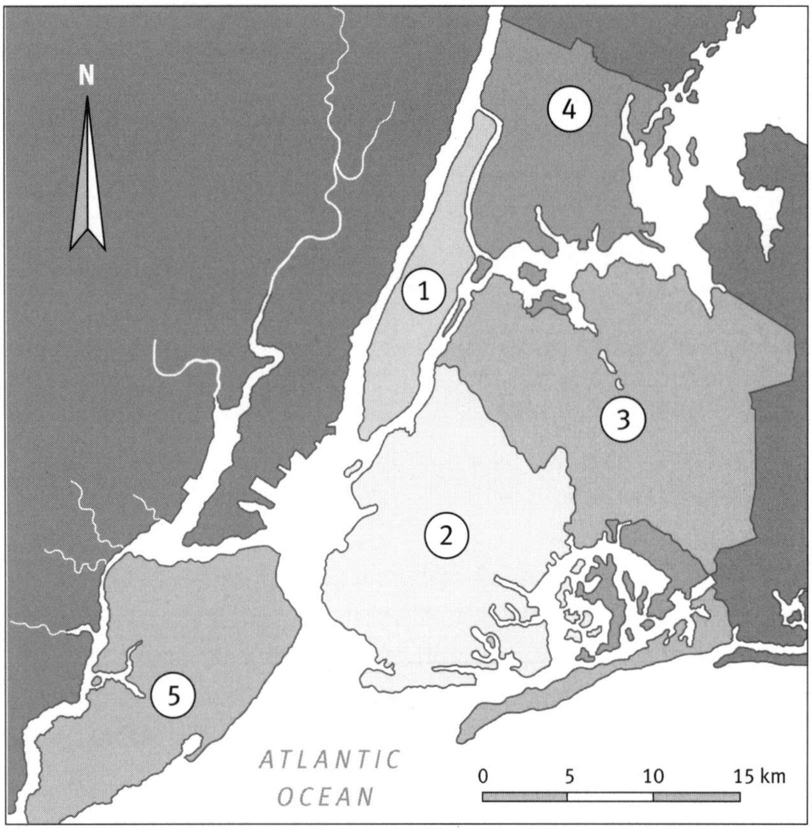

1 ______________________

2 ______________________

3 ______________________

4 ______________________

5 ______________________

Borough	Size	Inhabitants	Special facts/Sights

Can you now answer these questions? Practise with a partner.

What's the size of ______________________ ? – ________________ is ____ square kilometres.

How many people live in ________________ ? – _______ people live in ________________.

What are the special sights in ____________ ? – The special sights in _______ are ___________.

NYC SIGHTSEEING ADVERTS – PICTURES

In New York City you can go on a sightseeing tour by double-decker bus, boat, bike and even by helicopter!

- Read the adverts that describe the different tours and match them with the right pictures (cut the pictures out of this page and glue them onto the correct adverts on the next page).
- Search for the adjectives in the text that describe the nouns on worksheet C2 and fill them in.

Materials: worksheet C1 "NYC Sightseeing Adverts", pictures of the adverts on this page, scissors, glue, answer key, worksheet C3 "Find the Right Adjective"

NYC SIGHTSEEING ADVERTS – TEXTS 1

C

If you're a fan of the movies, you shouldn't miss this tour!

Guided by a New York actor or actress, this two-hour tour will take you through the city to see where scenes from movies like *Home Alone, When Harry Met Sally* and *Wall Street* were shot! You'll be entertained with the interesting facts and scenes from classic and contemporary movies.

Sturdy shoes are recommended for this unforgettable tour!
The tour price of only $ 33,95 includes bike rental fees and tour escort.
Departure: daily at 10 am and 1 pm.

A

Welcome to New York City!

Explore the incredible architecture, including the world's most famous buildings on our sightseeing tours. Seeing Manhattan and Brooklyn has never been so convenient! Whether you're going to Times Square, the Brooklyn Museum or Harlem, enjoy our hop-on, hop-off service at over 50 stops, day and night!

Duration: 2–3 hours
Price: $ 45.00

NYC SIGHTSEEING ADVERTS – TEXTS 2

D

Enjoy a 3-hour cruise to discover the secrets of New York City!

You'll sail around Manhattan Island and see three rivers, seven major bridges and all five boroughs.

A magnificent close-up of the Statue of Liberty is guaranteed!

Beverages, food and traditional souvenirs are available on board.

Time:
9.30; 10.00; 10.30; 11.00; 12.00; 14.30

Adult: $29 Child: $17

B

Explore Manhattan's famous skyline from high above!

You will explore the impressive Statue of Liberty, Ellis Island, The Empire State Building and many other inspiring attractions in only seven minutes!

Our sightseeing tours are available at Manhattan Heliport from Monday to Friday (excluding holidays) from 9:00 am to 6:30 pm.
Saturdays from 9:00 am to 5:30 pm.

Adult: $56 Child: $36

FIND THE RIGHT ADJECTIVE

1. a ______________________________ skyline
2. the ________________ Statue of Liberty
3. ______________________________ facts
4. ____________________ and ________________ movies
5. ______________________________ clothes
6. ______________________________ shoes
7. a ______________________________ close-up
8. the ____________________________ architecture
9. ______________________________ attractions
10. an ________________ tour
11. the world's ____________ buildings
12. ______________________________ souvenirs
13. ______________________________ bridges

PREPARED FOR MEETING MISS LIBERTY?

- Work with a partner.
- Read the text "The Statue of Liberty".
- Look up the new words in a dictionary and write them into your exercise book.
- Cut out the statement cards from the next page. Take one of them. Read the statement on it to your partner and ask him if the statement is right or wrong. If it is wrong, ask your partner to correct it. If his answer is right, he can keep the card.
- Change roles.
- Count your cards. Who is the winner?

Materials: text "The Statue of Liberty", dictionary, "right and wrong" cards

The Statue of Liberty

The Statue of Liberty on Liberty Island in New York Harbor is certainly one of the main attractions of New York City. It was a symbol of freedom and hope for hundreds of immigrants who arrived on Ellis Island in the 1860s. The statue is also called Lady or Miss Liberty and it was a present from France to the people of the United States and still symbolizes the friendship between the two nations. "She" arrived in 350 pieces in 214 boxes in New York Harbor on June 17, 1885 on board of a French ship. "Her" construction was finished in 1886 and Lady Liberty officially celebrated "her" 100th birthday on October 28, 1986. 289 steps lead from the bottom to the top of the right arm with the torch which is 46.5 metres above the base. There are seven rays on "her" crown that represent the seven continents. In her left hand "she" holds a tablet with the roman numerals "July 4th, 1776", the day that marks America's independence from Britain. A poem on the base written by the American poet Emma Lazarus, who was born in New York City, reads as follows:
"I lift my lamp beside the golden door" –
the door to freedom and hope.

A CARD GAME: RIGHT OR WRONG?

Right or wrong? The Statue of Liberty is a symbol of freedom and hope. **Right**	**Right or wrong?** The Statue of Liberty was a present from Germany to the people of the United States. **Wrong:** The Statue of Liberty was a present from France to the people of the United States.
Right or wrong? The Statue of Liberty arrived in New York on board of an American ship. **Wrong**: The Statue of Liberty arrived in New York on board a French ship.	**Right or wrong?** The Statue of Liberty is also called "Liberty Island". **Wrong**: The Statue of Liberty is also called "Miss Liberty" or "Lady Liberty".
Right or wrong? The 50th anniversary of the Statue of Liberty was celebrated on October 28, 1986. **Wrong**: The 100th anniversary of the Statue of Liberty was celebrated on October 28, 1986.	**Right or wrong?** The seven rays on the crown of the Statue of Liberty represent the seven days of the week. **Wrong**: The seven rays on the crown of the Statue of Liberty represent the seven continents of the world.
Right or wrong? The Statue of Liberty holds a tablet in her right hand. **Wrong**: The Statue of Liberty holds a torch in her right hand.	**Right or wrong?** The poem on the base of the statue saying "I lift my lamp beside the golden door" means: *Ich erhebe mein Licht neben der goldenen Pforte.* **Right**

MISS LIBERTY'S SECURITY GUIDELINES

Imagine you want to visit Lady Liberty with your class. To prepare your visit your teacher has given you the security guidelines for the area and he wants to be sure that you understand them all.

- Work with a partner.
- Each one of you takes a worksheet and folds it (vertically) in half. One looks at text A (English) and one of you at text B (German).
- Translate the English text into German. Your partner can correct you.
- Change roles.

A

1. There must be one teacher or adult chaperone for every ten students.
2. Students must remain with their chaperons all the time.
3. Food and drink may not be consumed anywhere within the Statue.
4. Chewing gum is not permitted. Please deposit chewing gums in trash cans.
5. Anyone who is caught damaging or in any way vandalizing this national monument will be subject to a fine or arrest.

B

1. Jeweils zehn Schüler müssen von einem Lehrer oder einer erwachsenen Begleitperson beaufsichtigt werden.
2. Die Schüler dürfen sich nicht von ihrer Begleitperson entfernen.
3. Das Essen und Trinken ist im Gesamtbereich der Statue verboten.
4. Das Kaugummikauen ist nicht erlaubt. Bitte die Kaugummis in den Mülleimern entsorgen.
5. Jede Beschädigung oder Zerstörung dieses nationalen Denkmals wird zur Anzeige gebracht und mit einer Geld- oder Gefängnisstrafe geahndet.

YOU CANNOT PLAN THE WEATHER

(so it's better to plan your tour)

You are planning a sightseeing tour in New York City but you are waiting for the weather forecast to decide if you want to go on a sightseeing tour by helicopter, boat, double-decker bus or bike.

- Look at the pictures and make up plans by using *if-clauses*. Write down your sentences. Compare them with the answer key.
- Remember: We use the simple present in the *if*-clause and the *will*-future in the main clause if it is **possible** to fulfil a **condition.**

Materials: worksheet C5, answer key

Key to weather symbols:

It's cloudy

It's windy

It's sunny

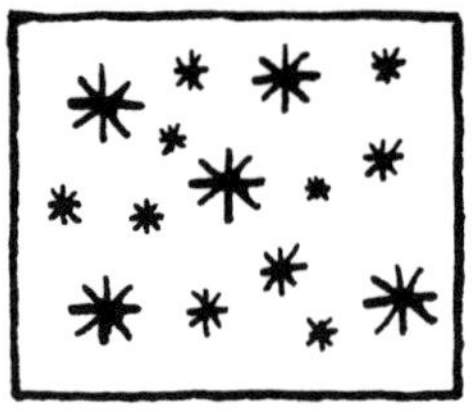

It's snowing

It's raining

WORKSHEET

Example:

If it's raining, I will not go sightseeing by bike, I will go sightseeing by bus.

1. ______________________________

____

2. ______________________________

____

3. ______________________________

____

4. ______________________________

____

A GUIDED TOUR

You are on a sightseeing tour in New York.

- Do you understand what your guide tells you? Look up the words you do not know in the list on worksheet D2 to be sure you understand the guide. Fill in the missing words and compare your completed list with the answer key.
- Listen to the guided tour on a double-decker bus through New York City and follow the route of the tour on the map (map: below; printed text: D3).
- Have a look at the pictures of the four sights on worksheet D4 and glue the right picture beside each sentence.
- At Station D5 you can win with adjectives!

Materials: worksheet D2 "Vocabulary list", dictionary, answer key, cassette, cassette player, worksheet D3 with pictures of sights in New York, descriptions of sights in NYC, scissors, glue and answer key

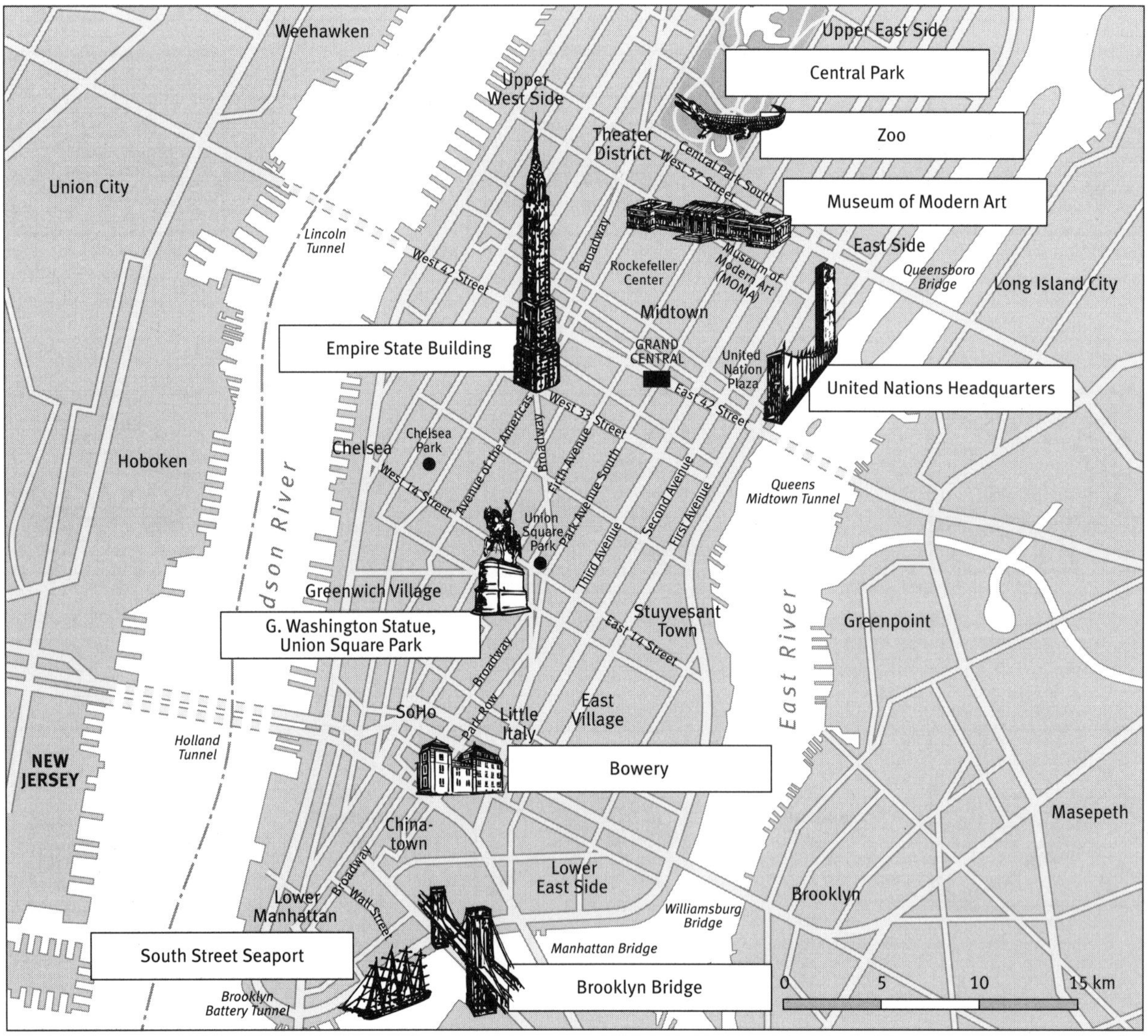

WORKSHEET: VOCABULARY LIST

ENGLISH			GERMAN		
Noun	Verb	Adjective	Noun	Verb	Adjective
pedestrian walkway	______	______		______	______
suspension bridge	______	______		______	______
statue	______	______		______	______
		impressive			
skyscraper	______	______		______	______
observation desk	______	______		______	______
elevator	______	______		______	______
floodlight	______	______		______	______
	illuminate				
administration		______			______
member state	______	______		______	______
headquarters	______	______		______	______
security force	______	______		______	______
	issue	______			______

WHAT THE GUIDE TELLS YOU

"Welcome to our sightseeing tour through New York City on a double-decker bus. Our starting point is Brooklyn crossing the East River on Brooklyn Bridge that leads us right into downtown Manhattan. The bridge is 1,825 metres long and 486 metres wide. The bridge has also a wide pedestrian walkway which is open to pedestrians and cyclists. When the bridge opened in 1883 it was the largest suspension bridge in the world. Perhaps you have seen the bridge in recent movies like *Night at the Museum* and *Superman Returns.*

Our tour continues on the Bowery up to midtown Manhattan passing China Town, Little Italy and Union Square Park. The park is popular for its impressive statue of George Washington, the first president of the USA. We're turning into East 34th Street to see the famous Empire State Building. When the skyscraper was completed in 1931, it was the tallest building in the world. After the World Trade Center was destroyed in the attacks of September 11, 2001 it is now once again the tallest building in New York. It raises to 381 metres on the 102nd floor and has an observation deck on the 86th floor. Visitors can go up there by high speed automatic elevators in less than one minute. The observation deck is open daily, 365 days a year. On a clear day you can see more than 80 miles! Floodlights in different colours illuminate the top of the building at night. The building can be seen in many classic as well as contemporary movies, for example in *King Kong, Spider-Man* and *Sleepless in Seattle.*

We're turning left towards the East River into First Avenue where you can already see the flags of all the member states of the United Nations which are displayed along the avenue. The United Nations Headquarters is located between 42nd Street and 48th Street. This is an international zone that belongs to all the 192 member states. The United Nations has its own security and fire forces and issues its own postage stamps. People from all the member nations work at the United Nations Headquarters. The United Nations Headquarters has four main buildings. The largest of the four buildings is the Secretariat, the home of the United Nations' administration. It has become a worldwide symbol of the United Nations.

Our tour now leads us to uptown Manhattan and will end in Central Park where you can continue your private sightseeing tour with a picnic or a visit to the Conservatory Garden or the zoo. You will also find two ice-skating rinks if you prefer a more energetic afternoon. If you prefer a cultural event, you can watch a stage play at the open-air theatre or listen to an open-air concert.

We have arrived at Central Park. Thank you for your attention and have a nice afternoon!"

SIGHTS AND DESCRIPTIONS

The bridge is 1,825 metres long and 486 metres wide. When it opened in 1883 it was the largest suspension bridge in the world. It is known from recent movies like *Night at the Museum* and *Superman Returns*.

It's home to a zoo and a garden. For sports events there are two ice-skating rinks. Here you can relax watching a stage play in the open-air theatre or listening to an open-air concert.

The United Nations headquarters is an international zone that belongs to all 192 member states. It has its own security and fire forces and issues its own postage stamps. The Secretariat is the largest of the four buildings.

When the skyscraper was completed, it was the tallest building in the world. Today it's still the tallest building in New York. Visitors can go up to the top floor by high speed automatic elevators in less than one minute. The building can be seen in many classic as well as contemporary movies, for example in *King Kong, Spider-Man* and *Sleepless in Seattle*.

Brooklyn Bridge

Central Park

Empire State Building

UN Building

WIN WITH ADJECTIVES!

- Cut out the cube below, fold it and glue it together. Now you have your own adjective dice.
- Find yourself a partner.
- Throw the dice and find a noun that you can describe with the adjective on the top. Try to think of a noun from one of the NYC texts you already know.
- Make up a correct sentence with this noun and this adjective in it. (Write your sentence down on an extra piece of paper.)
- Cross out this adjective on the list.
- Now your partner throws the dice, makes up a sentence (and writes it down).
- The winner is the person who first crosses out all the adjectives. (You will know who of you has got the most sentences right after your teacher has checked what you have written down.)

Materials: adjective dice, scissors, glue, adjective list, extra piece of paper

Adjective list:

famous – impressive – magnificent – comfortable – inspiring – interesting

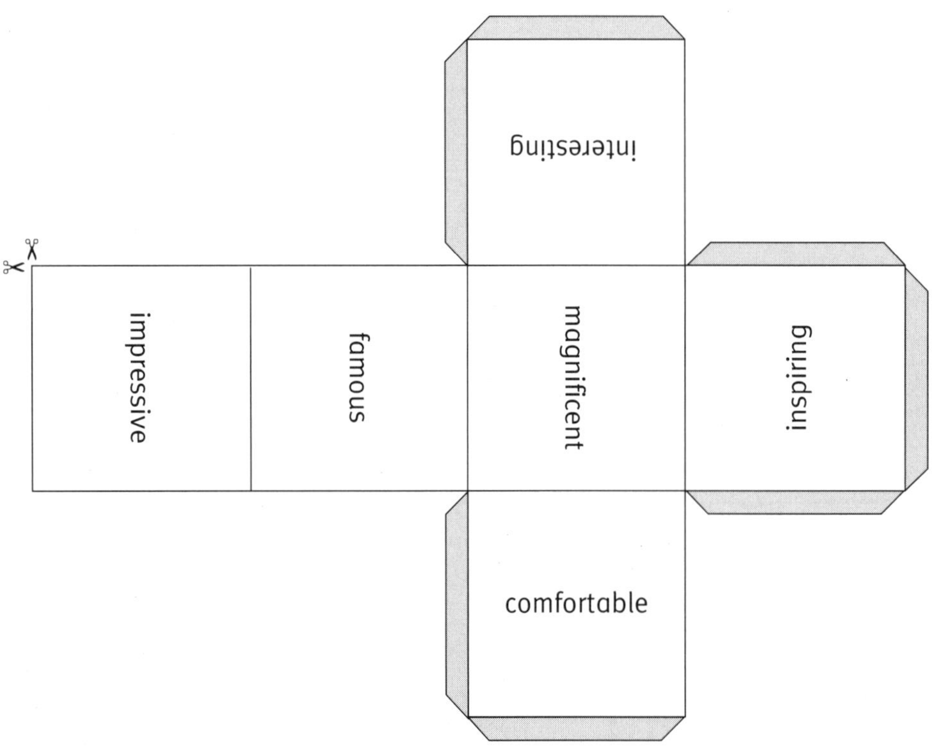

DESCRIBING THE WAY

- Find a partner.
- Have a look at the map of Manhattan (D1) and the four description cards.
- Read the first description of the way to your partner. Ask him to follow your description of the way on the map. If your partner follows your instructions correctly, he will end in front of a famous place or sight in Manhattan.
- Change roles now. Your partner takes the second description card and reads it to you.

You can use these phrases:

turn right into ...	*biege rechts ein in ...*
turn left into ...	*biege links ein in ...*
cross ...	*überquere ...*
walk down ...	*laufe ... hinunter*
walk up ...	*laufe ... hinauf*
pass ...	*gehe vorbei an ...*

Route 1 Coming from the Metropolitan Museum of Modern Art you walk down Fifth Avenue. Then turn left into East 42nd Street. You cross United Nations Plaza. Now you are in front of a building. It is the ...? United Nations Headquarters	**Route 2** You're at Grand Central Station. Walk down East 42nd Street, crossing Fifth Avenue. Go straight on, now it's West 42nd Street. Turn right and walk down the Avenue of the Americas. Go straight on. After you have passed West 57th Street and Central Park South you are in front of ...? Central Park (South Entrance)
Route 3 You're at Union Square Park. Turn right and walk down West 14th Street up to the Avenue of the Americas. Turn right and walk up this avenue. After crossing Broadway you are in front of New York City's highest building. It's called ...? Empire State Building	**Route 4** Coming from Wall Street you go up Broadway until you reach Union Square Park. Turn right and walk a few steps down East 14th Street. Then take the first left and walk up Park Avenue South. Past East 42nd Street you are at ...? Grand Central Station

THE MOST POPULAR SPORT IN NYC

- Read the text about the most popular sport in New York City.
- Look up the new words and write them into your exercise book.
- Try to find out the German expressions for the baseball phrases from the text. You can use your dictionary or try to find them on the internet. Write them down on worksheet E2. Compare your translations with the answer key.
- Complete the sentence beginnings in the table (E3). Find the correct answer card for each field of the table. Put the cards face down* on the fields.
- If you have put the answer cards down correctly, you will now see a picture. Do you know what it shows?

* face down= *verkehrt herum; hier: mit der Schriftseite nach unten*

Materials: text: "Baseball", dictionary or computer with internet access, word-cards, board

BASEBALL

The most popular sport in New York City is baseball. The origins of this game are not clear but some historians say that it has its roots in earlier bat-and-ball games* brought to America by British and Irish immigrants.
New York City has two famous professional baseball teams: The New York Yankees and the New York Mets. The stadium of the New York Yankees is located in the Bronx.
The game is played by two teams of nine players each on a field with four bases that is formed like a diamond. Alternately a pitcher (defense) of each team pitches (throws) a hard leather covered ball towards a batter (offense) of the opposing team who tries to hit the ball with a wooden bat. At the start of the game, the home team pitches and the players of the visiting team bat. If the batter hits the ball, his team scores runs by running from base to base. The starting base is called the home base. The defending team tries not to let the batting team get any runs by defending the field and getting control of the ball. The team that has the most runs is the winner.
Being such a popular sport, baseball has even influenced American everyday language. Expressions such as "to touch base with somebody", "to throw someone a curve", "to go to bat for someone" or "to keep your eye on the ball" all have their origins in baseball slang.

*bat-and-ball games: games that are played with a bat and a ball

BASEBALL VOCABULARY

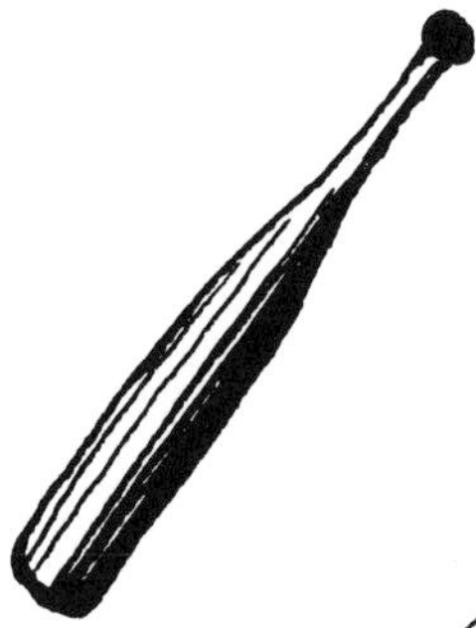

bat

ball

baseball glove

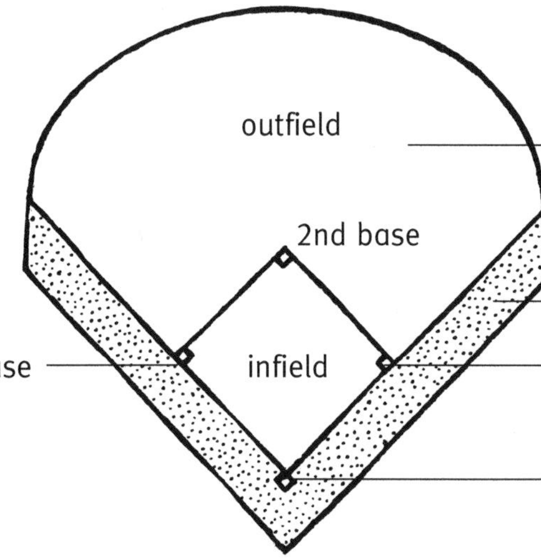

parts of a baseball field

batter

pitcher

Baseball expressions in everyday language:

(a) to touch base with somebody

____

(b) to throw someone a curve

____

(c) to go to bat for someone

____

(d) to keep your eye on the ball

____

ARE YOU A BASEBALL EXPERT? – SENTENCE BEGINNINGS/QUESTIONS

The New York Yankee stadium is located in this borough.	One of the professional American baseball teams	Games that are played with a bat and a ball are called ...
The baseball field is formed like a ...	The player who throws the ball is called a ...	The player who hits the ball is called a ...
Baseball language has influenced American ...	The starting base in a baseball game is called the ...	The batter hits the ball with a ...

ARE YOU A BASEBALL EXPERT? – ANSWER CARDS

The Bronx	The New York Yankees	bat-and-ball games
batter	pitcher	diamond
everyday language	home base	wooden bat

JIGSAW FOR BACK OF ANSWER CARDS

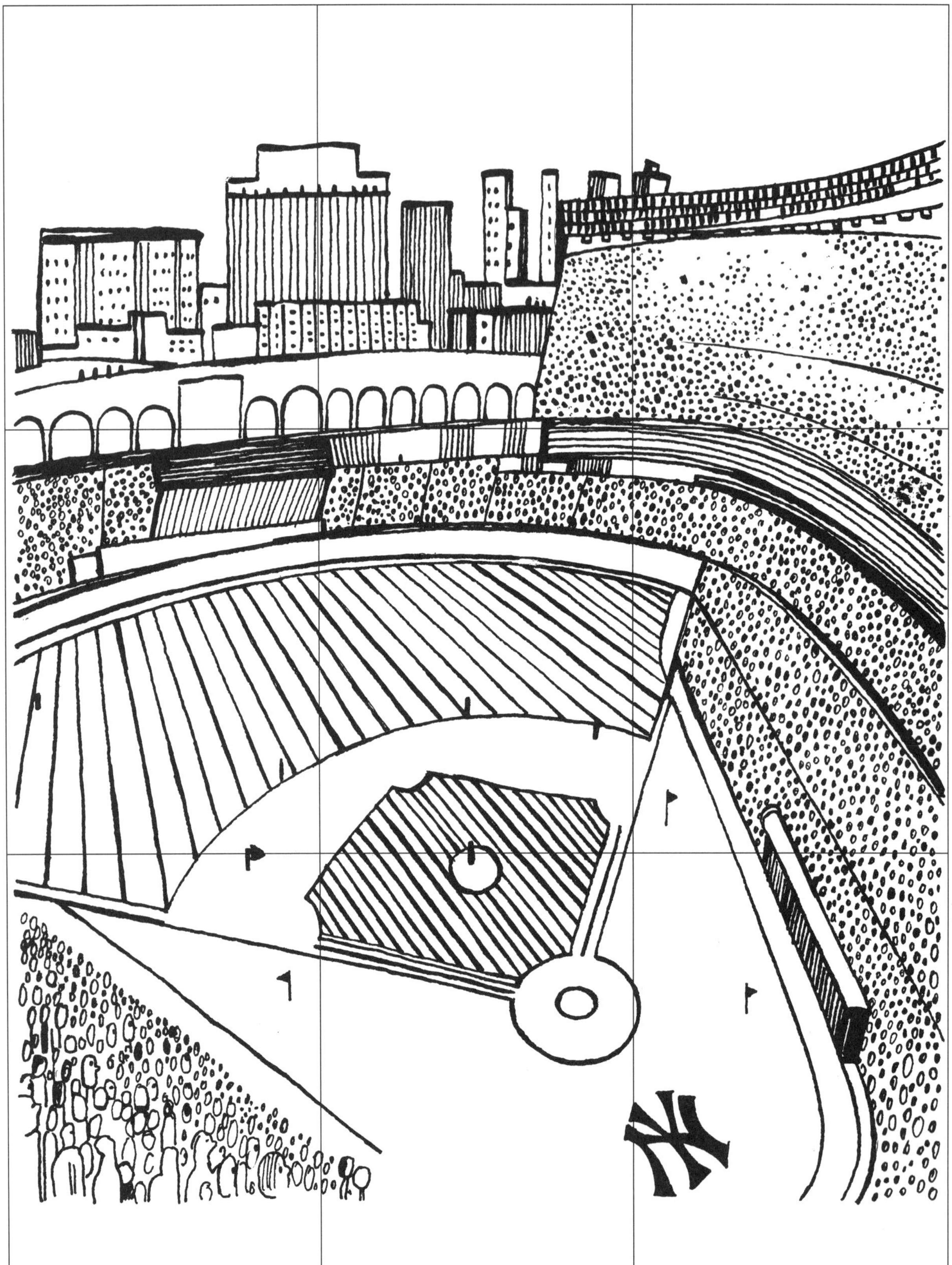

THE NEW YORK CITY MARATHON

- Read the text about the New York City Marathon.
- Look up the new words and write them into your exercise book.
- Mark the route of the marathon on the map. Compare it to the answer key.
- Answer the questions on the text. Write the answers into your exercise book and compare them with the answer key.

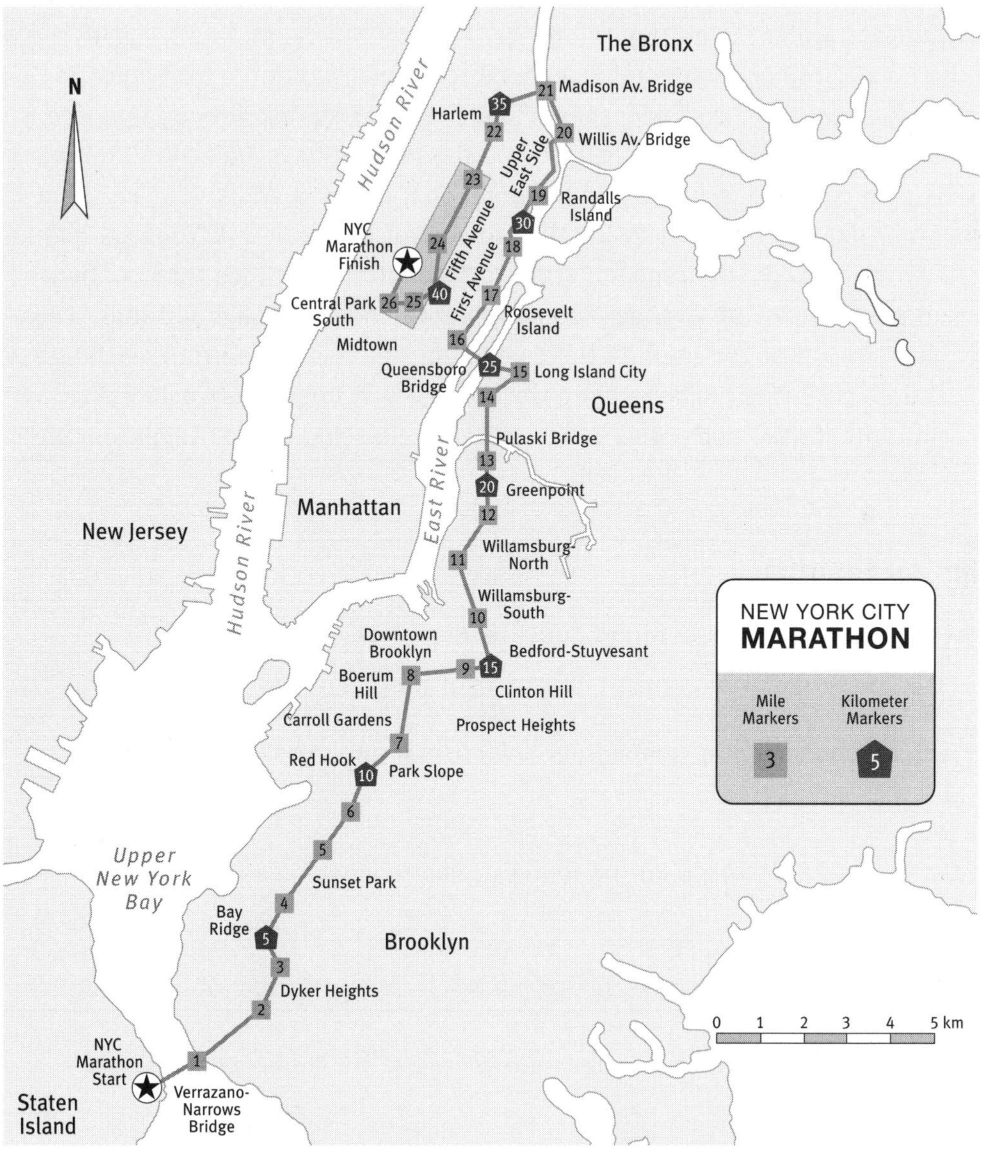

TEXT

The New York City Marathon

It is the world's most famous annual road running race over a distance of 26.2 miles. This marathon always takes place on the first Sunday of November. The first New York City Marathon was held in 1970 in Central Park. Only about one hundred spectators watched the 127 competitors running through the park and only fifty-five runners crossed the finishing line. Today this marathon is a spectacular event that attracts amateurs as well as professional competitors from all over the world. With 37,866 finishers in 2006, it was also the largest marathon race ever run. The course begins on Staten Island near the Verrazano Narrows Bridge which is closed to road traffic for this event. After the bridge, the course continues through Brooklyn passing Bay Ridge, Sunset Park, Boerum Hill, Bedford-Stuyvesant, Williamsburg (South and North) and Greenpoint. At 13.1 miles the runners cross the Pulaski Bridge, and enter Queens. After about two and a half miles in Queens, they cross the East River on Queensboro Bridge leading to First Avenue and into Manhattan. The climb up to this bridge is considered the most difficult point in the whole marathon. The race continues north on First Avenue and, crossing Willis Avenue Bridge, the runners enter the Bronx. After passing the stadium of the New York Yankees and crossing Madison Avenue Bridge, the runners return to Manhattan. The race then continues through Harlem down Fifth Avenue leading along the Museum Mile and into Central Park. At the southern end of Central Park the competitors run along Central Park South where the spectators cheer the runners during the last mile. At Columbus Circle the runners enter Central Park once again and finally cross the finishing line at Tavern on the Green.

QUESTIONS ON THE TEXT:

1. At what place and in which borough does the marathon start and end?

___

2. How many boroughs do the competitors have to run through?

___

3. How many and which bridges do the runners have to cross?

___

4. Have a look at the map. Which rivers do the runners have to cross?

___

POPULAR ABBREVIATIONS

The American language is full of abbreviations that are also used for short messages.

- Find out the meaning of the short message.
- Poetry that really adds up*! Read the poem by Michael Rosen and try to 'translate' it into its 'long' form. Compare your solution with the answer key.
- Write a short message for a classmate or your own poem on an extra sheet and collect them on a poster in the classroom. The short message abbreviations key below will help you.

* to add up: *(1) rechnen, addieren; (2) aufgehen, einen Sinn ergeben, „hinhauen"*

What does this short message mean: 2DAY WE WILL GO2NYC2C MY FRIENDS

Michael Rosen

UR 2 GOOD
2 ME
2 BE
4 GOT
———
10

SHORT MESSAGE ABBREVIATIONS KEY

- 0 – nothing
- 2 – two, to, too
- 2DAY – today
- B – be
- 4 U – for you
- B4 – before
- BC – because
- BRO – brother
- BT – but
- C – see
- D8 – date
- EZ – easy
- GF – girlfriend
- GR8 – great
- HOLS – holidays
- L8 – late
- L8R – later
- R – are
- SIS – sister
- U – you
- UR – you are
- A3 – anyplace, anytime, anywhere
- B4N – bye for now
- CUL – see you later
- FYI – for your information
- HAND – have a nice day
- HRU – how are you
- JK – just kidding
- MU – I miss you.
- NP – no problem
- PCM – please call me
- RUOK – are you OK?
- Thk U – thank you
- XLNT – excellent

AMERICAN AND BRITISH ENGLISH

In the United States some expressions differ from those used in the United Kingdom. We speak of American English (AE) and British English (BE).

- Put the small triangles together. Match the AE expression on one side of the first triangle and the corresponding BE word on one side of the second. (Use a dictionary if you are not sure.)
- Go on until you have matched all the sides of all the triangles.
- If you put all the triangles together correctly, they will form a bigger triangle again.
- Compare your solution with the answer key.

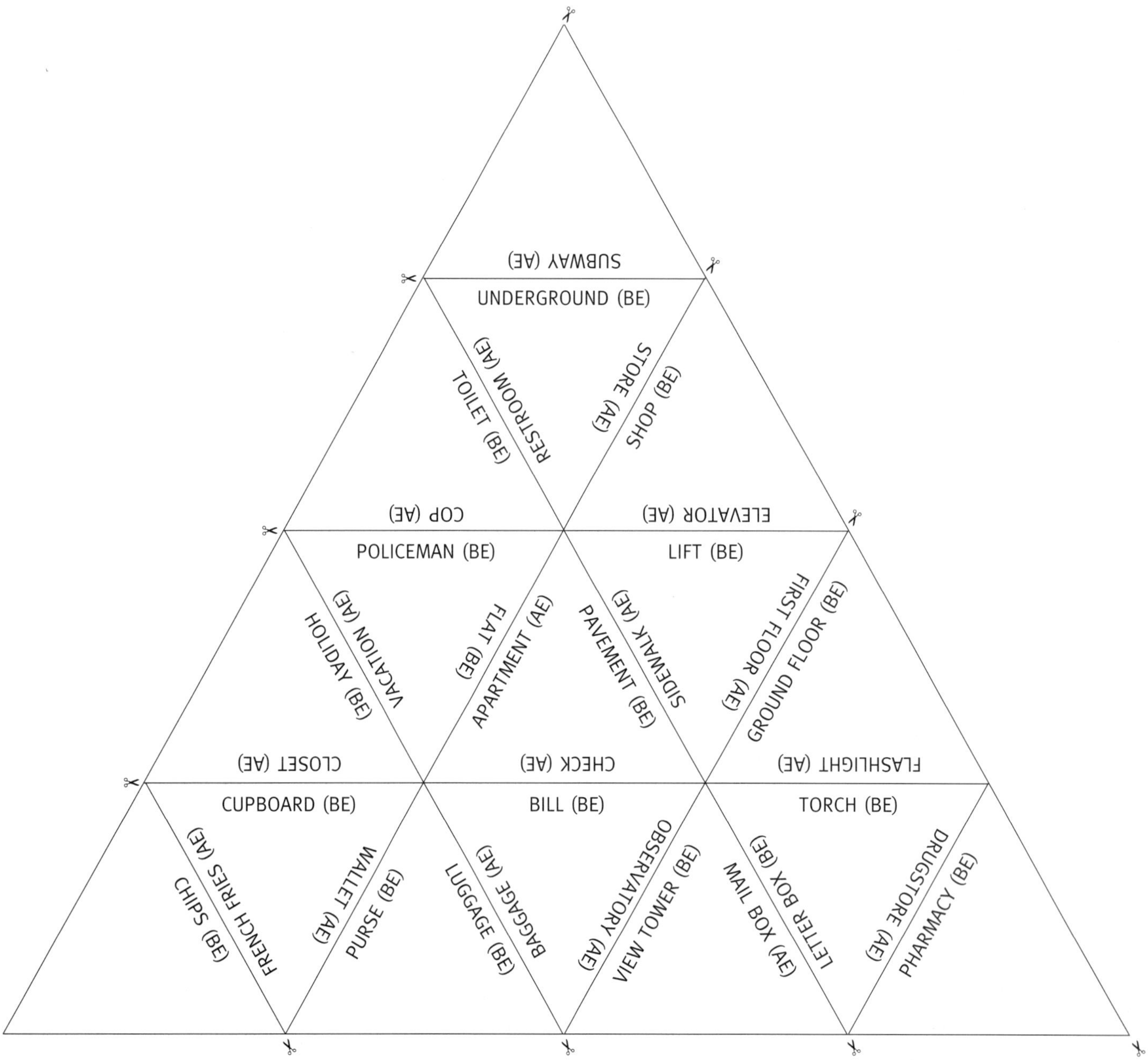

A NEW YORK CITY ACROSTIC

- Show what you know about the "Big Apple" and write an acrostic*.
- Collect all your acrostics on a poster in the classroom.

* An *acrostic* is a poem or other piece of writing in which usually the first letters of each line can be read downwards to form a word or words.

Example:

Boroughs

I ______________________________

G ______________________________

A ______________________________

P ______________________________

P ______________________________

L ______________________________

E ______________________________

GAME: A TOUR THROUGH NEW YORK CITY

Material: A dice, two game pieces and 33 answer cards

RULES OF THE GAME:

- Play with a partner.
- Throw the dice and move forward the correct number of spaces.
- If you land on a space, answer the question.
- If you land on a picture, name the sight shown.
- Your partner checks your solution by looking at the answer key. If your answer is correct, throw the dice again.
- The one who reaches the end of the board first is the winner.

When you see this picture, take the bus and move foward two spaces.

You've lost your bag on your sightseeing tour. Throw the dice again and move back the according number of spaces.

Joker! Miss Liberty will help you. Take a joker. You can use it if you don't know the answer to a question.

Cut out these cards and use them as jokers if you don't know the answer to a question.

GAME: A TOUR THROUGH NEW YORK CITY

1 The most populated borough of New York is ...	**2** A large urban park in New York City. It appears in many movies and television shows.	**3** Where did the first immigrant who arrived on Ellis Island come from?	
8 Who was the first president of the USA?		**6** Put this sentence into the passive: *The New York City Road Runners organize the New York City Marathon.*	**5** This bridge connects Brooklyn with Manhatten Island and is one of the oldest suspension bridges.
9 The Yankee Stadium is located in this borough.	**10** Find another word for "famous".		**12** When it was completed in 1931 it was the tallest building in the world. Today it's still the tallest building in New York City.
16 Which of New York City's boroughs ist the most famous? Why?	**15** Right or wrong? The seven rays of the crown of the Statue of Liberty represent the seven days of the week.		**13** What it the most popoular sport in New York City?
17 Name three adjectives to describe an attraction in a city.		**19** Finish the following sentence: The cityscape of New York City is dominated by ...	**20** What does the expression "keep your eye on the ball" mean in German and where does it come from?
24 This museum is housed in the building that immigrants to the United States once came through.	**23** Translate the following sentence: *Students must remain with their chaperons all the time.*		**21** Give one reason why an immigrant arriving on Ellis Island had to return home.
25 This statue is a symbol for freedom and hope. It was a present from France to the people of the United States.		**27** What is the nickname of New York City?	

MY FAVOURITE STATION

After you have finished all the stations, fill in the card "My Favourite Station" and collect all your cards on a poster in the classroom.
Have a look at the cards on the poster and discuss your opinions with your classmates.

MY FAVOURITE STATION

Name ________________________________

My favourite station was number ______.

At this station I learned something new about ____________________________.

This information was interesting for me because ___________________________.

I would still like to know more about ___________________________________.

A2

English		Deutsch	
NOUN	**VERB**	**SUBSTANTIV**	**VERB**
immigrant	*immigrate*	*Einwanderer*	*einwandern*
arrival	arrive	Ankunft	ankommen
hope	hope	Hoffnung	hoffen
escape	escape	Flucht	flüchten
persecution	persecute	Verfolgung	verfolgen
check	check	Überprüfung/Prüfung	(über)prüfen
return	return	Rückkehr	zurückkehren
danger	endanger	Gefahr	gefährden
rejection	reject	Ablehnung	ablehnen

A3

1						I	M	M	I	G	R	A	N	T	S								
2									S	T	A	T	U	E	O	F	L	I	B	E	R	T	Y
3						I	R	E	L	A	N	D											
4					D	I	S	E	A	S	E												
5							H	U	N	G	E	R											
6				O	P	E	N	E	D														
7					H	A	R	B	O	R													
8									F	R	E	E	D	O	M								
9					H	E	A	L	T	H													
10								M	E	N	T	A	L										
11									A	N	N	I	E	M	O	O	R	E					
12	R	E	G	I	S	T	R	Y	R	O	O	M											
13							M	U	S	E	U	M											

Ellis Island is also called:

I	S	L	A	N	D	O	F	T	E	A	R	S
1.	2.	3.	4.	5.	6.	7.	8.	9.	10.	11.	12.	13.

A4

Name: *Mac Gowan*
First name: *Emma*
Date of birth: *July 29, 1894*
Last permanent residence:
Country: *Ireland*
Town: *Connacht*
Final destination: *Manhattan*
Reason for leaving: *poverty, searching a job*

B2

2. mistakenly = incorrectly
   another name = a synonym
3. guide = lead
4. the view of a city = cityscape
   tall buildings = skyscrapers
5. ethnic variety = ethnic diversity
6. another country = foreign country
7. population increase = population growth

B3

A	P	P	L	E		P	I	E
1.	2.	3.	4.	5.		6.	7.	8.

B4

1 Manhattan; 2 Brooklyn; 3 Queens; 4 The Bronx; 5 Staten Island

Borough	Size	Inhabitants	Special facts/Sights
Manhattan	88 km²	1.5 million	Most famous and most densely populated borough, most tourist attractions are located here, Empire State Building, UN Building, Union Square, Central Park
Brooklyn	251 km²	2.5 million	Brooklyn Bridge, most populous borough in NYC
Queens	462 km²	2.2 million	John F. Kennedy Airport, Flushing Meadows Corona Park
The Bronx	149 km²	1.4 million	Birthplace of rap and hip hop, Yankee Stadium, Bronx Zoo
Staten Island	266 km²	444 thousand	"The forgotten borough", Staten Island ferry which passes the Statue of Liberty

C1

A – 4

C – 2

D – 3

B – 1

C2

1. a *famous* skyline
2. the *impressive* Statue of Liberty
3. *interesting* facts
4. *classic* and *contemporary* movies
5. *comfortable* clothes
6. *sturdy* shoes
7. a *magnificent* close-up
8. the *incredible* architecture
9. *inspiring* attractions
10. an *unforgettable* tour
11. the world's *most famous* buildings
12. *traditional* souvenirs
13. *major* bridges

C5

1. If it is cloudy, I will not go sightseeing by boat, I will go by bus.
2. If it is snowing, I will not go sightseeing by bus, I will go by boat.
3. If it is sunny, I will not go sightseeing by bus, I will go by bike.
4. If it is windy, I will not go sightseeing on a helicopter, I will go by bus.

D2

English			German		
Noun	**Verb**	**Adjective**	**Noun**	**Verb**	**Adjective**
pedestrian walkway	–	–	*Bürgersteig*	–	–
suspension bridge	–	–	*Hängebrücke*	–	–
statue	–	–	*Statue*	–	–
impression	*impress*	impressive	*Eindruck*	*beeindrucken*	*beeindruckend*
skyscraper	–	–	*Wolkenkratzer*	–	–
observation deck	–	–	*Aussichtsplattform*	–	–
elevator	–	–	*Aufzug*	–	–
floodlight	–	–	*Flutlicht*	–	–
illumination	illuminate	*illuminated*	*Beleuchtung*	*beleuchten*	*beleuchtet*
administration	*administrate*	–	*Verwaltung*	*verwalten*	–
member state	–	–	*Mitgliedsstaat*	–	–
headquarters	–	–	*Hauptquartier*	–	–
security force	–	–	*Sicherheitskraft*	–	–
issue	issue	–	*Ausgabe*	*herausgeben*	–

D4

E2

to touch base with somebody – *mit jemandem in Verbindung treten*

to throw someone a curve – *jemanden auf dem falschen Fuß erwischen*

to go to bat for someone – *sich für jemanden einsetzen*

to keep your eye on the ball – *seine/die Augen offenhalten*

E4

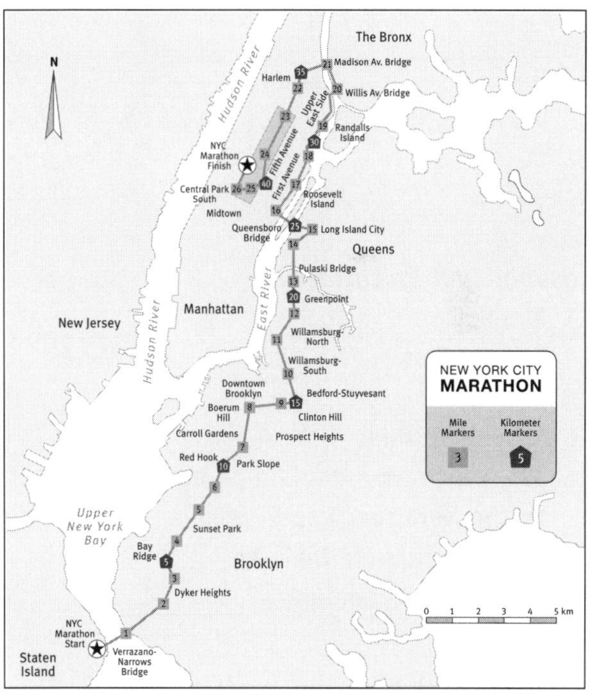

1. The NYC marathon starts on Staten Island near the Verrazano Narrows Bridge and ends in Manhattan at Tavern on the Green.
2. The runners have to run through all five boroughs.
3. The runners have to cross five bridges: the Verrazano Narrows Bridge, Pulaski Bridge,

Queensboro Bridge, Willis Avenue Bridge, Madison Avenue Bridge.

4. The runners have to cross the New York Upper Bay and East River.

F1

Today we will go to New York City to see my friends.

You are too good
to me
to be
forgotten.

F2

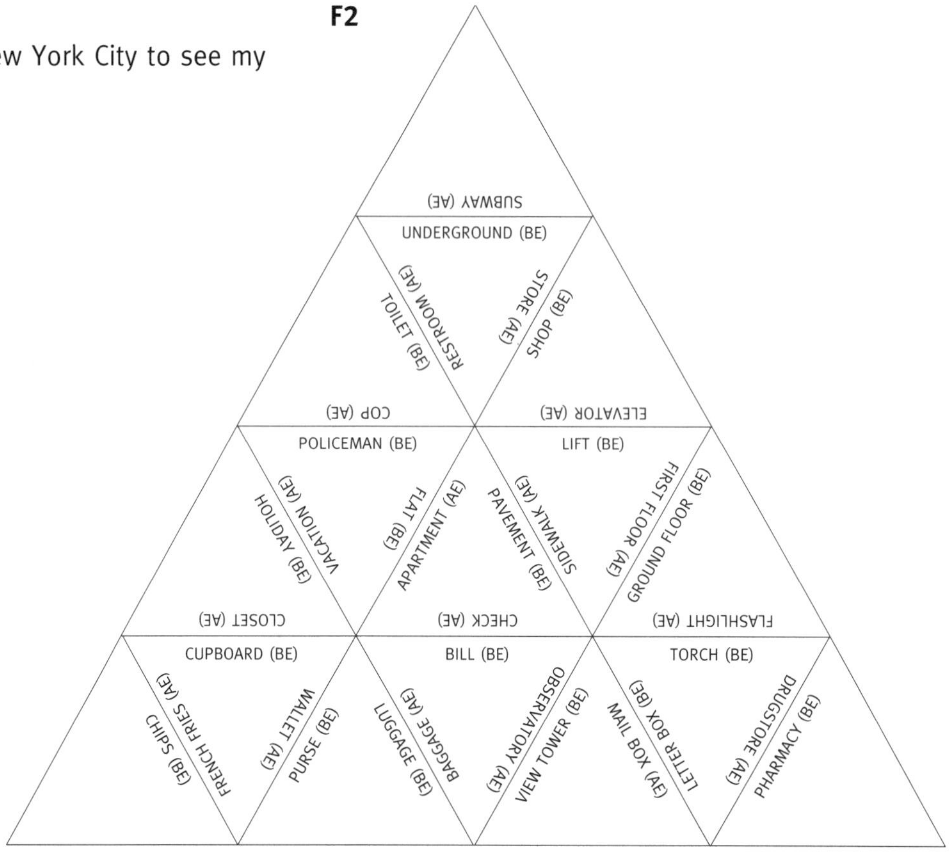

G1

Lösungen für Spielfelder:

1 Manhattan
2 Central Park
3 Ireland
5 Brooklyn Bridge
6 The New York marathon is organized by the New York Road Runners.
7 The Empire State Building
8 George Washington
9 The Bronx
10 well known
12 The Empire State Building
13 Baseball
14 The UN-Headquarters
15 Wrong. The seven rays represent the seven continents.
16 Manhattan. The most popular sights of NYC are in this borough.
17 famous, popular, well-known, magnificent, impressive ...
19 skyscrapers
20 It comes from baseball language and means: *Halte deine Augen offen!*
21 a contagious disease that could endanger public health or a criminal background
23 Die Schüler dürfen sich nicht von ihrer Begleitperson entfernen.
24 Ellis Island Immigration Museum
25 The Statue of Liberty
26 Brooklyn Bridge
27 The Big Apple
28 The Statue of Liberty